PENGUIN BOOKS

MY FELLOW PRISONERS

Mikhail Khodorkovsky was Russia's leading businessman and an outspoken Kremlin critic. Born in 1963 in Moscow, he founded one of Russia's first private banks, Menatep. Group Menatep subsequently acquired a majority interest in the Yukos Oil Company. Under Khodorkovsky's leadership, Yukos revived the Russian oil industry, becoming one of the largest oil companies in the country, and the most transparent. He began sponsoring programmes supporting civil society through the Open Russia Foundation, funded several opposition parties and publicly challenged the Kremlin on the issue of corruption.

When he was arrested at gunpoint in 2003 he became Russia's most famous political prisoner. In 2005, Khodorkovsky and his business partner Platon Lebedev were convicted on fraud and tax evasion charges, sentenced to ten years and sent to Siberian penal colonies. Yukos was forced into bankruptcy and its assets were appropriated by a state oil company. Before becoming eligible for early release, new embezzlement charges emerged. Despite the fact that the charges contradicted those of the first trial, Khodorkovsky was put on trial again, and, in December 2010, sentenced to fourteen years in prison. The trials were heavily criticized by the international community. Intellectuals such as Elie Wiesel

began to campaign for his release. Amnesty International declared Khodorkovsky and Lebedev prisoners of conscience, 'trapped in a judicial vortex that answers to political not legal considerations'.

While imprisoned, Khodorkovsky fought for the rights of his fellow prisoners, going on hunger strike four times. Despite risks to his own safety, Khodorkovsky continued to speak out and write extensively about both the injustices he saw around him and his vision for Russia. He was pardoned on 20 December 2013 and, upon his release, vowed to continue fighting for prisoners' rights.

My Fellow Prisoners

MIKHAIL
KHODORKOVSKY

PENGUIN BOOKS

PENGUIN BOOKS

Published by the Penguin Group
Penguin Books Ltd, 80 Strand, London WC2R ORL, England
Penguin Group (USA) Inc., 375 Hudson Street, New York, New York 10014, USA
Penguin Group (Canada), 90 Eglinton Avenue East, Suite 700, Toronto, Ontario, Canada M4P 2Y3
(a division of Pearson Penguin Canada Inc.)
Penguin Ireland, 25 St Stephen's Green, Dublin 2, Ireland (a division of Penguin Books Ltd)
Penguin Group (Australia), 707 Collins Street, Melbourne, Victoria 3008, Australia
(a division of Pearson Australia Group Pty Ltd)
Penguin Books India Pvt Ltd, 11 Community Centre, Panchsheel Park, New Delhi – 110 017, India
Penguin Group (NZ), 67 Apollo Drive, Rosedale, Auckland 0632, New Zealand
(a division of Pearson New Zealand Ltd)
Penguin Books (South Africa) (Pty) Ltd, Block D, Rosebank Office Park,
181 Jan Smuts Avenue, Parktown North, Gauteng 2193, South Africa

Penguin Books Ltd, Registered Offices: 80 Strand, London WC2R ORL, England

www.penguin.com

First published 2014
001

Copyright © MBK IP Limited, 2014
All rights reserved

The moral right of the author has been asserted

The letters in this volume first appeared in Russian in *The New Times*, and are
published here by kind permission of M. Khodorkovsky/MBK IP Limited.

Set in 11/13pt Bembo Book MT Std
Typeset by Jouve (UK), Milton Keynes
Printed in England by Clays Ltd, St Ives plc

Except in the United States of America, this book is sold subject
to the condition that it shall not, by way of trade or otherwise, be lent,
re-sold, hired out, or otherwise circulated without the publisher's
prior consent in any form of binding or cover other than that in
which it is published and without a similar condition including this
condition being imposed on the subsequent purchaser

ISBN: 978-0-141-97981-6

www.greenpenguin.co.uk

Penguin Books is committed to a sustainable
future for our business, our readers and our planet.
This book is made from Forest Stewardship
Council™ certified paper.

Contents

Foreword

or

How I wanted to write about my impressions of a classical music concert

There were many times in prison, and later in the camp, and then again in prison, and then again in the camp, when I really wanted to listen to a live performance of classical music. Somehow it just never happened; life was a bit crazy, I suppose; there was a lot going on. I also yearned for a situation where I could read, and discuss what I had read with someone – a real person – instead of having to converse much of the time with a sheet of paper. And now it seems I have absolutely no desire to write about that other life of mine, the prison life.

But a pertinacious editor has asked me to write a foreword to a book that was created in conditions far removed from those in which I find myself today.

This has not proved the easiest of tasks, because, when reading through what I've written over the previous ten or more years that I was in prison, I involuntarily find myself re-experiencing that life over and over again, a life that once seemed as though it would go on for ever.

On 25 October 2003, the day of my arrest, it would never have occurred to me that details of what I remembered, even the most trivial and mundane, would be of interest to anyone. So, I survived – what more is there to say? Besides, as an out-and-out technocrat, not in the least oriented on the humanities, I had always regarded reading as primarily an essential tool for obtaining the information I needed, or for forcing myself to think about something. In fact, even now, hand on heart, I can honestly say to myself: well what kind of writer are you, anyway?!

Do I remember the details of my arrest? Not particularly. Or, rather, I do remember that I was thinking about something completely different from what all the wonderful books they give us to read in school say you should be thinking in such a situation.

I remember I didn't feel anger; I was too stubborn for that. Though it wasn't a question of stubbornness either. Confusion, a sense of uncertainty – these are entirely alien feelings for me.

I was thinking about my parents, my wife, my children. I was trying to figure out what would happen to the company. I was definitely thinking about how there might be interrogations using psychotropic drugs, as had happened to my colleague Alexei Pichugin – how they would slip something into my food, do a video recording. Which is why at first I tried not to eat, and to drink very carefully, although I wasn't frightened – this I can say for sure . . .

It is a strange and wonderful feeling to be able to type out letters and words on a computer, and abandon the habit of jotting things down on little pieces of paper at odd moments of the day or night.

I was often asked – and continue to be asked – how many

times a day, week, month or year I had the opportunity to use the internet, a computer, and other such blessings of technological progress. Well, I'll tell you: for over ten years I never once had such an opportunity! Some of today's opposition leaders were genuinely amazed at how well informed I was in our correspondence; they refused to believe that I didn't have a computer or internet access in my cell. And they continued to be amazed, right up until that moment when they themselves ended up in a cell for a couple of weeks – then they understood . . .

What you are now holding in your hands is an attempt to show a world that is beyond the comprehension of most people – a world from the past, in which some live in comfort and others do not; a world that coexists in my country with the real world, but where it's as though technological progress and the achievements of civilization have never happened. But everybody in Russia – irrespective of whether they have read Solzhenitsyn and Shalamov or have no idea who these great writers are – knows almost on a genetic level, deep in the subcortex of their brains, the saying *ot sumy da ot tyurmy ne zarekaisya*: you can't prevail over begging bowl or jail.

Relying on the internal discipline that my parents had instilled in me since childhood, not allowing myself to think about getting out anytime soon, I kept my mind occupied by writing numerous letters and engaging in intellectual disputes with distant opponents. And I wrote prison stories. About the things I saw myself or had learned about from others, things that can happen to anybody. I wrote about the country in which our remarkable people continue to live in penury and without rights. And I wrote about a future Russia that we will be able to feel proud of without a trace of shame – the Russia that will ultimately take the road of European civilization. A road we all share.

'That's them over there'

It's well known that prison is a place where you encounter the most unusual people. Over these past years a great swathe of humanity, with fascinating stories to tell, has crossed my path.

The feeling of wasted lives being thrown on the dust-heap is often overpowering. Human destinies ravaged, whether by themselves or by the soul-destroying system. I'm going to try to tell you about a few of these people and their situations. I have inevitably changed names and some details, given the circumstances of the people I'm writing about, but the essence of their characters and the situations they find themselves in are kept as I heard and perceived them myself.

After so long in prison I certainly have no illusions about the people I have come across. Nonetheless, many prisoners have their principles. Are they valid ones from society's point of view? Some are, some aren't. But they are principles, all the same, for which people are prepared to suffer. Really suffer.

It so happened that prison brought me into contact with a thirty-year-old guy on trial for suspected drug dealing.

Sergei is a long-term drug addict, though you wouldn't know it from his appearance. He looks a bit younger than his years, very spry, educated. His mother is a Gypsy, his father

Russian, which created an interesting situation, culturally speaking. His mother had to leave the Gypsy community, and she now works as a radiologist in a hospital.

Sergei speaks Roma, he knows Gypsy traditions and socializes with other members of the community, but doesn't feel part of it. He's been a drug-user for a long time (like most of the young people in his small town), but because he comes from a family of medical professionals and is strong-willed he is meticulous about the purity of the 'wares'; he also makes sure he eats properly and regularly detoxes – abstaining for several weeks to prevent a constant build-up of his tolerance levels.

In fact, he asked to be put in my cell so that he could go through one of his detox sessions, since the rest of the prison, he says, is not 'conducive to this'. For a few days he has a rough time, but then it eases up and he tells me his story, little different from dozens of others I've heard. As a user he would buy from one particular dealer; the police insisted that he grass on his supplier, he refused, so they fitted him up as a supposed dealer himself. Now he's back and forth to court where they'll likely give him between eight and twelve years even though he's never dealt. They planted some 'traced' money on him; where the drugs came from isn't clear.

I've heard so many of these stories. I nod politely, and that's the end of the conversation.

A few days later Sergei suddenly comes back from court in a state of shock. It turns out that they produced as a witness the person who had set him up. This guy's about fifty years old. He too was arrested, on some unrelated charge, and was given a medical in the prison hospital, where it was discovered that he had an incurable illness. This man gets into the witness box, recounts his situation, and declares that 'with my sentence, I'll die in jail. I'll be dead soon. I've a lot of sins on my conscience and I don't want to take on another one. So I'm going to tell the truth, and I'm not afraid even if they kill me.'

And then for forty minutes he tells everything about the set-up, how he was dealing drugs on the orders of the police, how he gave them the money, how they got rid of competitors and their clients, and so on. People crowd into the courtroom from the corridor, everyone listening to this chilling confession in deadly silence. Then the witness points at the investigators sitting opposite and says, 'That's them over there.' The investigators get up and try to leave, but the court usher doesn't let them, saying 'The judge may want to take you into custody.' The judge then stops the proceedings and clears the courtroom.

A few minutes later Sergei's lawyer enters his cell and says that the judge is calling them back in. 'What do you want me to ask for?' the lawyer says.

'My freedom, what else?'

'That's not going to happen,' the lawyer replies and goes out.

An hour later he comes back in. 'They're offering you six years.'

'Not good enough.'

The lawyer leaves again, but returns almost immediately. 'Three years. You've already done more than a year, you'll be out on parole.'

'Done.'

'What next?' I ask Sergei.

'Three years, I'm being sentenced tomorrow. Maybe I should have held out to the end?'

'No, Sergei, you did the right thing. The system doesn't work any other way.'

With 'tomorrow' comes his 'three-year' sentence, and the application for parole. He assures me that he will go back to his job as a railway worker and quit the drugs. I wish him luck.

So that's the system. That's the kind of people they are. They go to the very limit, to the edge. Which one day awaits us all.

Kolya

It so happened that I met a young man, Nikolai (Kolya), as he was about to be released. There was nothing particularly remarkable about Nikolai. He was doing time for a fairly straightforward crime, drug possession – like roughly half the rest of the country's prison population.

It was clear that he would be back. He'd already spent five of his twenty-three years behind barbed wire and showed little intention of changing his ways in the future. Although clearly not stupid, Kolya had grown up feeling rejected and unwanted. His life had been a constant battle with this feeling of rejection while being surrounded by similar outcasts.

Six months later I met Kolya again, now with a grisly scar on his stomach.

'Kolya, what happened?'

'Ah well, they got me with some gear again.'

For a moment Kolya hesitated, but then told me the full story, which is later corroborated by others who had witnessed it. Having taken in a repeat offender, the police investigators decided to charge him with an extra crime, for good measure. This kind of bargaining goes on all the time and is usually fairly open: you'll only get an additional couple of years, they say, if we ask the judge, but you'll have to carry the can for some robbery – and you'll get extra visiting rights or choose where you end up. Generally it's nothing more than a mobile phone robbery or some such. Kolya, after not much thought, agreed. But then for the identity parade they brought in an old woman whose purse, containing about 2,000 roubles, had been snatched by some scum. The pensioner clearly remembered little about it and quickly 'identified' the person indicated by the investigators.

At which point Kolya suddenly dug in his heels. 'I've never touched an elderly person in my life, only people my own age. Robbing an old woman of her last rouble – no, I didn't sign up for that, and I won't do it. Whatever you do to me!' The investigators were dumbfounded. 'Kolya, as far as the law's concerned there's no difference. The money is the same, so's the sentence. Why are you getting so steamed up? We can't go and turn all of this around just because you're feeling sensitive about it.'

'I won't do it,' said Kolya.

So they sent him back to his cell, 'to think it over' – having first given him a bit of a beating, 'as is only right and proper'.

After a while he knocked on the cell door from inside; when they opened the food hatch – his guts came flying out. Kolya had 'opened himself up', and some. Full-on hara-kiri. The scar is as wide as a finger and stretches half-way across his belly.

While the doctors were rushing across, others in the cell tried to stuff his entrails back in again.

It was a miracle they saved him. Now he's disabled, but he has no regrets. 'If they'd gone and pinned that old woman's purse on me, I'd have died anyway,' says Kolya – meaning the loss of his self-respect, without which his life is unimaginable.

I look at this man who has been sent down so often and think with a certain bitterness of the number of people on the outside who hold their honour far less dearly than he, who wouldn't see anything particularly bad about robbing an old man or woman of a couple of thousand roubles. Although their crime would be clothed in clever words. They have no shame.

And, like it or not, I feel proud of Kolya.

Alexei's Story

These days there are very strong feelings against paedophiles among the public, which is not surprising. It's an appalling crime, the result of a depraved and twisted mind that believes itself to be above the law.

Politicians, as is their wont, will use any situation to try to boost their ratings. But the 'quota system' (whereby people are arrested to meet a predetermined level of arrests), given the lack of genuine judicial protection, has resulted in abuses that are no less appalling and have tragic outcomes.

I got to know a guy who was doing time for a paedophilia-related crime and who was consistently refused all requests for parole and a reduced sentence.

Alexei had ended up in prison at the age of nineteen. He's now twenty-two — a nice young guy who doesn't have any tattoos or other 'peculiarities' that often characterize prisoners. He's hard-working and does amazing things on the old metal-turning lathe.

His story is simple. As a teenager he was given a suspended sentence for robbery. It was pretty run-of-the-mill — he had one too many, nicked a mobile phone from an acquaintance, an hour later found himself in custody. He got four years suspended.

To this day he gets very embarrassed when I call him a 'bandit' and ask him to explain why he did it.

He's clearly ashamed about the whole thing, and doesn't even want to talk about it.

Two years went by; he was still going to school. Aged eighteen he met a girl, Ira, at a disco. She was underage. They started living together, at her parents' home. They hoped to get married as soon as they could. But then the campaign against paedophilia started. The town they lived in wasn't big, everyone knew everything that went on. The local police officer received his 'quota' demand, and so he went into action. The parents of the girl wrote letters, the bride-to-be sobbed in the courtroom, but it was all to no avail. The judge 'understood everything' but she too had a quota to fill and a campaign to adhere to.

The result: five years, taking into account the suspended sentence.

It was the minimum sentence the judge could impose, if you ignore the fact that the verdict was completely unfair in the first place.

For two years Ira waited for Alexei. They hoped that the court would reconsider his case, that he would be released on parole. But, alas, it became clear that none of these bureaucrats was prepared to go against the grain.

Even visits were impossible.

After two years Alexei wrote to Ira telling her not to wait for him. And he stopped replying to her letters.

I look into his eyes. No, there are no tears, just a well-hidden, deep-rooted despair.

He's a strong, good-natured guy, like so many other strong, uncomplicated people. They took away not just his freedom but also his happiness. He doesn't complain, he accepts those who are his seniors, his 'bosses', as a force of nature. He was caught up by a wave and thrown on to the shore – alone, without a home, without a family.

What can you do?

But I am left feeling angry and bitter about this hopelessness, about the cruelty of our system, about the cries of people who don't want to know the truth and demand only one thing: 'Crucify him!'

Everyone needs to stop; look around you! Not everything is that simple and unambiguous.

During my time in prison I've met a good number of such unfortunate people. Some of them have their partners waiting for them. They have a long wait. Some get married in prison. Children come along. And the fathers are still there behind bars, condemned as 'paedophiles'.

What sort of people are we, if we allow such a thing?

'The investigation will get things straight'

When I read articles, letters or blogs I am often amazed at people's genuine belief in the integrity of the police and judiciary, and how their pronouncements and interviews are taken as a fairly reliable source of information.

I will admit, of course, that many representatives of these professions, in their personal lives, are entirely decent citizens who, like the rest of us, lie only occasionally – when they have to – and feel bad about doing so.

When they're at work and part of 'the system', however, they lie virtually all the time, and as a rule tell the truth only to gain someone's trust – which then enables them to lie more successfully afterwards. They lie to individuals, to the court, to one another. These are the rules of a system which, if for this reason alone, needs to be dismantled. It just isn't a place where honest people can function.

I happened to come across a rather interesting person in prison. A con-man, a member of one of the 'law enforcement' gangs. Led by a colonel serving as prosecutor, the gang comprised dozens of operatives, a customs officer, a few other people of official rank, a civilian intermediary (my new acquaintance) and a trader.

Its 'business' was of the standard kind: the customs officer would find out who had just received some merchandise at the warehouse, the prosecutor (as he then was) would initiate criminal proceedings, the operatives would 'arrest' the goods and pass them on to the trader who sold them at profit, whereas a notional cost was returned as 'compensation for the loss'.

While all this was going on, the owners of the property would be rotting away in jail; afterwards they would either be released or given the full treatment, depending on how 'perceptive' they'd proved to be.

And so it continued until one fine day when this particular cabal happened to stumble across a bigger racket than their own.

While the prosecutor slunk off to Armenia, and the operatives were released on bail, the civilian members of the group ended up in pre-trial detention. It's well known, after all, that 'ravens don't peck out other ravens' eyes'.

Despite what had happened, my cellmate still retained a steadfast faith in the 'law-enforcement agencies'. 'The investigation will get things straight' was his stock response to any flagrant abuse we might hear about from fellow inmates, or see on television.

At first this really got on everyone's nerves. In prison there just isn't anyone so naïve as to put their trust in 'the investigation'. But then I found a useful outlet for my cellmate's way of thinking. For example, when we watch a TV report on a police general's luxury residence worth millions of dollars – gilded toilets, piles of jewellery, the works – I immediately ask: 'How come nobody knew? He must have been paying off the top brass, surely? What's the investigation going to say?'

'The investigation will get things straight,' is my

cellmate's inevitable response. 'No doubt the money for the house was provided by the general's children who earned it honestly working in a state company; criminal elements who'd had their wings clipped by the general must have set him up, and the most he's guilty of is dereliction of duty.'

When I first heard this kind of reasoning, I assumed my cellmate was joking. But he was quite serious, and a couple of weeks later his version was confirmed by the official press secretary of the 'respected' Investigative Committee.

And so it went on. Whether it was the latest government bandit shown on TV or an article about a truly dreadful case like a drunk copper running over a woman and her child, my cellmate would declare that 'the investigation will get things straight'; and he'd come up with some totally absurd version of events (along the lines of 'they threw themselves under the wheels, and in any case he'd been dismissed from the force long before'). And soon enough this version would be officially confirmed. He got it right every single time.

But nothing lasts for ever. The time came for his verdict. None of us were surprised when the operatives got suspended sentences, the trader ten years, and my cellmate – fourteen.

The investigation had straightened things out all right . . .

But to say that to his face would have been cruel. Back in the cell, not a word was spoken . . .

After a couple of days the shock wore off and he sat down to lodge a cassation appeal, saying: 'It's okay, the investigation will get things straight.'

Soon after that he was transferred, but we heard on the prison grapevine that his sentence remained unchanged.

So when you're next watching television and hear the words 'criminal proceedings have been initiated' or 'the investigation has established', before you allow yourself even for a second to believe what's being said, just think: maybe the person who has written these words is a colleague of my cellmate, the con-man.

At any rate, in the regular announcements of the Investigative Committee's press secretary, I hear his voice loud and clear.

The Guards

I'm writing these notes because I want people who care about these things to know what I have personally experienced in prison.

Over time I've turned from an ordinary victim into an interested observer, and I've discovered that for many people the prison world remains *terra incognita*. And yet in our country one in every hundred people is currently in prison; one in ten (maybe by now one in seven) of the male population passes through prison at some point in their lives.

Moreover, prison has a terrible effect on the majority of both prisoners and guards. It's not yet clear, in fact, which group is affected more.

Society has to do something about this human tragedy. And for a start people need to know about it.

This story is about the guards.

The people who feel most uninhibited in prison are the police investigators, known in the vernacular as the 'operatives'. Their official duty is to prevent crimes that someone might be thinking of committing, and to uncover those that have already been committed. As a result they're not much constrained by prison regulations. Facial rearrangements and endless interrogations, mobile phones and drugs – these form just a small part of their standard arsenal.

The operatives usually know how to work with people and are good at it. They know how to talk, how to listen. But there are exceptions.

Take the head of the police investigation unit, a 27-year-old called Pelshe, whose first name and patronymic are so hard to pronounce that by common agreement he's long been known simply as Sergei Sergeyevich. He's not a man for small talk. He fixes his transparent, ice-cold eyes right into yours and lurches about desperately, caught in a verbal trap of harrumphing and interjections. When he's sober, that is.

In fact, he's rarely sober. When you see those slightly protruding ears glowing red like traffic-lights and catch that faint whiff, you know he's in a good mood and his speech will flow smoothly. But at the same time it's a signal to the unwary: 'Keep your mouth shut.' Alcohol has no effect on the professional operative's memory.

However, Sergei Sergeyevich is just as likely to treat the most taciturn prisoner to a dose of his none-too-gentle fists. He hits people like a true professional, leaving minimum trace, though the recipient spends a week groaning and pissing blood. But no one reckons this 'talking to' is particularly bad. The general opinion is that he's not an animal; 'freelance operatives' are far rougher.

As well as applying his fists, Sergei Sergeyevich can also treat you to tea and sweets, and give you cigarettes; he'll even let you make a call on his mobile. Though you can be sure he'll make a note of the number.

Sergei Sergeyevich regards the visits of ad-hoc commissions as an unavoidable evil, and his attitude is no different from that of the other inhabitants of the prison colony. In order to feed these numerous commissions, Sergei Sergeyevich generally collects funds from the staff. But if it's getting close to pay-day, then he might look for add-itional 'support' from the prisoners themselves.

The detainees take an understanding approach to the prob-lem and chip in. Sometimes, instead, they ask him to 'sell' back something previously taken from them, like their telephone or another forbidden item. And then the 'high contracting parties' reach a consensus, and a deal is struck.

Sergei Sergeyevich lies to the court and commissions without a second thought.

'Sergei Sergeyevich, who wrote this two-page explan-ation?' the judge asks.

'The convict Badayev, in his own hand,' replies Pelshe firmly. 'As is written.'

'But Badayev is illiterate; it says so in his personal case file. He only had two years of school!'

Sergei Sergeyevich says nothing, the traffic-lights glow red . . . You might think he's feeling embarrassed, but we all know the real reason. And Sergei Sergeyevich is lost in his own thoughts. He doesn't give a stuff about the court. The convict Badayev does give a stuff, but nobody else gives a stuff about Badayev.

In the difficult years of reforms, representatives of the criminal world (so-called 'overseers') kept the prisoners fed and prevented needless conflicts between them, while also embedding a criminal ideology. Now Sergei Sergeyevich and his colleagues do the same thing, effectively training up the future foot-soldiers of the criminal world.

'You're not a person, and those around you aren't people!'; 'You should just listen to your superiors and not think when following an order!'; 'The less you think, the better your life!'

These are the maxims that are hammered into the heads of 18- to 25-year-old detainees, and as a result the percentage that ends up back in jail is astronomical. Those who manage to stay out of prison do so in spite of it, not thanks to it.

In fact, this is why nobody is particularly surprised when a slightly more inebriated than usual Sergei Sergeyevich yells at the top of his voice at roll call: 'Who's the overseer here?! I'm the overseer!!!'

Indeed he is.

'Sergei Sergeyevich,' I ask him, 'if you and your colleagues were to change places with the prisoners currently in here, no one would notice much of a difference, would they?'

'They wouldn't,' he agrees, and seems not the least bit aggrieved by this state of affairs. He's the same as everybody else.

Sometimes, what takes place in prison seems like a version of ordinary life beyond the prison gates, just taken to a grotesque extreme. Nowadays in 'ordinary' life, too, it can be difficult to distinguish a racketeer from an employee of an official organization. In fact, does this distinction even exist for most people?

And what happens to those of us who are too frightened to stand up for our rights, who adapt and hide behind a mask of submissiveness? Does this protective mask not morph to become our real face? Do we not gradually turn into slaves, silent and unresponsive, but prepared to commit any abomination if so ordered from on high?

When I was leaving the colony, it was Sergei Sergeyevich who carried my things to the car.

'Please don't come back to our colony,' he said. 'It's more peaceful without you.'

Four years later the colony was burned to the ground, set alight by those same silent prisoners.

Guilty without Guilt: Volodya

It looks very likely that over the next few years we will find ourselves living in a bureaucratic-police state, with absolute power in the hands of a corrupt bureaucracy. A bureaucracy that's indifferent to our fate and utterly brazen. Here I want to tell the story of two people who have ended up in its clutches.

The cell door opens with its usual clank and standing on the threshold is a rather short, plump man with surprisingly long, slightly curly hair.

'Hello everyone,' he says and, limping heavily, makes his way over to a free bunk.

The young guy occupying the lower bunk sighs deeply, and gets up to switch places.

'It's okay, don't worry,' the small man says, clambering up using his stiff leg and unpacking his things like someone who's done this many times before.

Like all newcomers, he's left in peace for a few minutes to get his bearings, and then the cautious enquiries begin, and they continue over tea. It transpires that the guy – let's call him Volodya – has been in various prisons over the past few years, for the most commonplace offences.

Volodya turns out to be easy to get on with, one of those people who, in the business world especially, are adept at networking. Business intermediaries. In fact, that's exactly what he did before he ended up in prison.

Four years earlier, 'using his specific banking knowledge' (to quote his case file), he withdrew half a million dollars from the account of a member of a security agency, reckoning that, as the money was clearly dodgy, the guy wouldn't go to court.

But he had miscalculated. The bank reimbursed its client every last kopeck, and filed a suit. Volodya went down.

Truth to tell, this part of the story didn't bother him that much. He'd taken his chance, had blown it, and had been convicted without evidence – but not for nothing. Yes, his sentence was a bit heavy (eight years), but what could you do about that?

Having been sent to the prison colony, he started making plans for the future. After a couple more years he became eligible for parole. It was at this point, as Volodya related, that an order came through for him to be transferred to Moscow.

'I racked my brains and finally came to the conclusion that they were planning to stitch me up with someone else's bank fraud.'

What actually happened went far beyond his worst imaginings. The investigator declared that two years earlier he, Volodya, had beaten another detainee to death in prison.

My cellmates and I looked at each other, and then at little, lame Volodya, with a certain disbelief. Well used to this reaction, he pulled out his case file. Despite the fact that my own trial was ongoing, I couldn't resist reading it in its entirety. It was the story of yet another human tragedy – as terrifying as the Magnitsky case and just as commonplace in Russian prisons.

The file told the tale of a 45-year-old man who had ended up in prison because of a bottle of wine. An ordinary guy, he'd had a drink, wanted some more, didn't have any money, so walked into a supermarket and in an act of drunken stupidity grabbed a bottle from the shelf. Unfortunately this happened to be an expensive wine that had accidentally ended up on an open shelf. He was stopped at the till, the police were called and as the bottle cost more than 2,500 roubles he was sent to remand prison.

In prison his old ulcer flared up again and he was moved to the prison clinic where he spent a couple of weeks. After that he was transferred to another remand centre, again to its hospital facility. It was there, a week later, that they discovered that he'd broken nineteen ribs. And a week after that he died from injuries to his spleen.

So the cost of one stupid bottle of wine turned out to be a human life.

But where does Volodya come into this?

He was admitted to the same hospital as the man who died. But the hospital of the *first* prison!

A prison hospital (for those fortunate enough not to know) is essentially the same prison with the same cells, and, if you are recuperating in one cell, you might only find out what's going on in the other cells through prison correspondence.

The deceased man and our new cellmate never met – on this all the doctors and supervisors agreed unanimously. But this is by no means the biggest absurdity. The report stated that Volodya broke nineteen of the man's ribs with two punches. Anyone who has ever done any boxing or karate will tell you that this is impossible. It is quite possible, however, to break the ribs of a sick prisoner lying helplessly on the floor by stamping on them with heavy special-forces jackboots.

It's also impossible to transfer someone who's taken such a beating from one remand centre to another, moreover from one hospital to another, without anybody noticing anything. But then, as it turned out, it's entirely possible to ascribe the incident to another remand centre and thereby muddle everything up completely.

The case hung around for almost two years until circumstances aligned: a request not to release a man, and an old unsolved investigation . . .

After that it was just down to technicalities. You only need a couple of seasoned lags, one of whom had shared a cell with the guy who was killed, while the other had been in the neighbouring cell – and you explain their options in the simplest terms (either they pin it on the relevant person, or else . . .).

And so of course one of them 'saw' it happen, the other 'heard' it. And there you have it, bang to rights. Off to court!

The judge doesn't 'trust' the evidence of the doctors or the supervisors, or the log-book entries detailing transfers from cell to cell. Nor does he give any credibility to the doctors' notes and testimony that the deceased was transferred to the second prison without the injuries from a savage beating. But he believes sure enough the people who 'saw' and 'heard' it. They were specially brought in from a prison colony. So that's it. Guilty.

Over the past few days Volodya had been in a dire state. The investigators were trying to persuade him to confess, saying he wouldn't get much added to his sentence. But if he didn't, he'd get the full works.

He asked my advice. I confirmed that they weren't bluffing. But, beyond that, it was a matter for his conscience. And so Volodya refused to confess to the crime. He said to me: 'I wouldn't be able to look into the eyes of my friends, my family.'

My trial ended soon afterwards, so I only heard about the outcome of his case when I was already in Karelia. It was as predicted.

You might think that nothing like this could ever happen to you. After all, you don't go around stealing from supermarkets or siphoning money out of the accounts of police bureaucrats. But then, as our country's history goes to show, many have thought just the same, until it so happens that their highly desirable apartment has caught the eye of their neighbour-informer.

When people can be kicked to death, when courts are prepared to cover up crimes and convict the innocent, decent conduct is not the most convincing defence.

The Witness

I often find my thoughts returning to the question: what is conscience? How do we define what is 'good', and what do we feel ashamed of for the rest of our lives? When does conscience overcome fear, and when does fear overrule conscience?

Lyosha Badayev is an ordinary young Buryat guy from a remote village. He has a round, wide face and black narrow eyes, as if permanently squinting. He doesn't remember his parents; he was raised by his aunt. He only went to school for two years and then worked as a shepherd tending the communal flock.

One ill-fated day he tackled a thief who was trying to steal a ram. He threw a rock at him and hit his head, but the thief turned out to be a tough cookie and quickly came round. Lyosha, who had just run up to him, got frightened; he panicked and did something fatal – he hit him with the rock again. And then again.

Realizing what he had done, he abandoned the flock and made a run for it.

He was caught by chance a few months later, a thousand kilometres from home, when he tried to steal something to eat.

At his trial he was convicted of homicide – he got six and

a half years. A fair sentence, given all the circumstances. He was sent to a juvenile penal colony and then to adult prison.

I met Lyosha in the sewing workshop, where he'd found himself a refuge. He was a hard-working guy, quiet, inconspicuous.

A short time after, I was given a reprimand and I filed a charge against the administration. I was surprised to discover that Lyosha was summoned as a witness. I had no doubt that he would say whatever was expected of him. There are many methods of 'persuasion' available in the camp.

And so, the day of the trial. All the principal characters are assembled: the head of the camp, the head of operations, their deputies, with the chairman of the city court presiding.

Lyosha is called to the witness stand. He is clearly confused and frightened. He speaks hesitantly . . . but he speaks the truth! My lawyer and I exchange glances, not understanding what's going on. Our opponents look equally nonplussed.

The judge lets Lyosha stand down. He goes out of the door, but a moment later comes back in.

Lyosha points at the head of operations: 'He gave me two packs of cigarettes and told me to lie.'

I look at those sitting across from me. The screw is calm and composed on the outside, whereas his boss is slowly turning puce.

'But I wasn't going to lie, I told the truth. As for the cigarettes, here they are.'

And he hands the judge a pack of L&Ms, admitting, 'I smoked the other pack. I've never had cigarettes like these before.'

Everyone is struck dumb.

'So, I'll be going then, or do you need anything else?'

'Just go, you've said quite enough already,' bellows the boss.

Lyosha leaves; the dumb show continues.

At last the court chairman pronounces: 'Everything is in the court record. If anything should happen to this fellow, I'll make sure the record is made public.'

After the trial I go up to Lyosha.

'Why on earth did you do that? You know only too well there'll be trouble.'

He raises his squinting eyes. 'You haven't done anything bad to me. I couldn't do it.'

And he walks off.

Back to camp life and the inevitable payback. Sometimes, when coming out of the isolation wing, I'd learn that Lyosha was in there too. He'd been barred from the workshop. But whenever we happened to meet, he would smile and say, 'Everything's fine.'

Soon enough everyone in the camp came to hear all about what had happened. And when I asked to be informed immediately if anyone should try at any point to beat Lyosha (this being the usual practice), I got an astonished reply: 'Who would want to do that? The administration's afraid, other prisoners now respect him . . .'

Six months later I was moved to another prison. Lyosha's

term has now ended. What became of him? I don't know, and I don't want to enquire in case I cause him any trouble. But I hope very much that he goes through life with dignity and without fear.

We make a deal with our conscience: we lie, keep quiet, don't 'notice' things for the sake of a quiet life, we hide behind the interests of our nearest and dearest. We justify ourselves, saying that 'these are the times we live in', that 'everyone else is the same'.

But whom, in fact, are we striking that deal with? And how will we know when 'the other party' – our conscience – has refused it? Is it only when we end up facing adversity ourselves?

Or is it when we're near the end and we make that final reckoning of our lives, agonizingly aware that the time for 'dodging the raindrops' is over and all we have left is memory? But surely by then it is too late to change anything.

The Investigator

One of the most important people in the life of every prisoner is the investigator, the person on whom, given the realities of our judicial proceedings, your fate depends.

It's the investigator who uncovers or fails to uncover evidence demonstrating that a crime might have been committed; who designates whether you're the accused or the witness; who decides whether to arrest you or allow you bail on condition of not leaving the town; who even determines whether to allow a visit from relatives. And as a general rule all of this (and a great deal besides) is in the hands of a very young (under thirty), newly qualified law-school graduate.

According to the law the investigator is independent, almost as much as the judge. But in actual fact he is just a cog in the law-enforcement hierarchy – a small-time bureaucrat, who often doesn't even have a say in some of the key aspects of his work.

For four years, almost continuously, I have had to deal with these people. In fact, there was no requirement on their part to look as though they were investigating anything at all, but we were still required to spend many hundreds, if not thousands, of hours in the same room. It wasn't possible to avoid these meetings altogether, nor was there any particular reason to do so.

I encountered all kinds of investigators: those who were indifferent and felt burdened by their role, those who tried to understand something of the case, and those who were simply putting in the hours.

I bear no ill feeling towards any of them, so this story is loosely based on discussions with those who are no longer part of the system.

Yury Ivanovich was an unusual person in 'my' investigation team, most of whom were of non-Russian ethnicity. People like him are always a problem for their bosses because they're independent, or as independent as they can be within the parameters of the system. For Yury, a sense of his own worth was bolstered by a recognition of a certain self-sufficiency in his professional and daily life. A good education, an apartment inherited from his parents, and a lively mind allowed him sometimes to express his own opinion about operations he was involved in that were unrelated to my own case.

Occasionally he would even share these opinions with me.

One day Yury Ivanovich could barely contain himself. 'Can you imagine, Mikhail Borisovich, yesterday we had a police raid on illegal timber extraction!'

I could quite easily imagine such a thing. Forests are being decimated in a barbaric way, as close as possible to towns and roads, with the best trees being felled any old how and, of course, without proper permits which would have to be paid for. The timber is then smuggled across the border. This is how most of the local elite make their living.

'They call us in for the briefing,' he continued, 'and show us on a map where the plots of the police and other bosses are (i.e. where not to stick our noses in), allocate our areas of responsibility, and off we go. We get there and they're sawing away, ignoring us completely; they don't have proper licences, trees are being felled willy-nilly. We detain them and impound their equipment. The foreman just laughs and says, "I've already made a call to the right place, by the way." Half an hour later, we get a call: release the men, release the equipment, tear up the reports. The poachers laugh at us as we head off, totally humiliated. It turns out this "strip" belongs to the governor, and he hadn't even marked it on the briefing map. And then we get back to find all hell's broken loose, they're threatening to withhold our bonuses and so on. How can you do something like that? This is Siberian pine, after all, and there's so few left now . . .'

I hear genuine hurt and indignation in the investigator's voice. What's particularly pleasing is that it's not the potential loss of his bonus that's upsetting him. It's the humiliation he's been through, and the genuine concerns of a local inhabitant for his part of the world, that have pierced the armour of indifference to unfettered corruption.

We discuss the reasons for what has happened, and possible responses. I can tell that he has already thought this through a number of times, and now it's all just spilled out. Or maybe he's hoping that I'll come up with some unexpected answer.

Unfortunately I don't have such an answer. You either come to terms with it and enjoy the benefits, and feel like a piece of shit, or else you fight it, in the realization that they'll cover you with shit from head to toe.

Those are the rules of the game, in our system.

But there is another way out, and Yury Ivanovich took it. He handed in his resignation. Is this really the solution though? Because this raises another important issue: the process of 'negative selection', whereby gradually only the worst people remain in the system. Those who don't have the intelligence to understand what's going on, and those who do understand but don't have enough of a conscience to refuse to become part of it.

So idiots and lowlife – great material for building up the machinery of state.

And yet this is indeed our state.

The Grass

Arkady Bondar is a tall young guy with a broad smile that lights up his handsome face. He'll go up to every newcomer, when they're sitting dejectedly on their bed in the new arrivals' barracks, and strike up a conversation about life, or the reason they've ended up at the camp . . . Only a very naïve person will keep up the conversation. But the new arrival feels a need to talk, and there are plenty of naïve people around.

Other detainees in the barracks will watch what's going on with disapproval, but they don't get involved.

For Arkady is an 'official' grass; he works as an orderly in the Operations Division. Which means that he's nominally responsible for ensuring that the building is kept clean and tidy. But, in fact, he does something else entirely. He's a 'tongue-loosener' who tries to extract information about any crimes or accomplices the new arrival might have kept quiet about during his investigation.

But even this isn't his main task. His core 'business' is finding out who has banned stuff in their possession. Anything hidden during the search – money, playing cards, a sweater – lands the unsuspecting owner fifteen days in the isolation cell, and earns Arkady a carton of cigarettes or permission to use an otherwise banned iPod.

It's not a good idea to cross him. You might just find that, when it comes to the next routine search, those same playing cards mysteriously turn up in your bag.

So everyone keeps their mouths shut, exchanging meaningful looks instead. An experienced detainee will understand, while the rookie – well, what can you do, such is his fate. A bit later, when everyone's got to know each other and worked out who's who, we discuss Arkady and point out a further three grasses, operating further undercover than him . . .

But for now Bondar disengages himself from his victim, having had his fill. Result! He's found something out, the leech. And now he'll run off to grass on the guy. Sure enough, there he goes . . .

Incidentally, for a small fee Arkady will fetch you something from the visiting room, or even buy back from the officers something that's been confiscated.

He usually gives me a wide berth. But now I see him whispering something to my neighbour, who then comes up to me.

'Borisich, how do you spell "discrediting"?'

'Why do you want to know?'

'Bondar's asking.'

'Bondar, come here, will you?'

He comes over, avoiding eye contact. He's clearly scared. His parole is coming up and getting into an argument with me is the last thing he needs.

'Why do you want to know this?'

'The officers asked me.'

'Asked you what?'

'To write that you are discrediting the administration. But I don't know the word.'

'Get out of my sight.'

That evening I go and see the officers.

'You should at least think about whom you're giving these errands to.'

'Come on, Mikhail Borisovich, you know the kind of people we have in here,' they reply, not embarrassed in the least. 'We have to work with what we've got.'

We part with a few facetious remarks. I've won this round. But they're not in any hurry.

To most Russians, grassing people up is a deeply immoral business. Unlike the Germans or Americans, who regard 'informing the authorities' as something sacred. In our country informers have devastated millions of innocent lives. Almost every family has its victim of the repressions. The hatred of informers is engrained, sometimes even subconscious. Like coals covered with a dusting of ash, just blow on them and they'll flare up again . . .

In the camps, though, such behaviour is made the norm. In some cases it works, in others less so. These kinds of people are useful for the administration. But how on earth are they going to live when they're released? With values that society finds unacceptable.

We all know that sometimes you have to report what you've seen for everyone's safety, and sometimes in order to ensure justice.

But to inform on someone for a handout – that's worse than stealing. In Russia the informer's true reward is the utter contempt of those around him.

And you know something? I'm very glad my country is still like that.

As for Bondar, I heard of him again about two years later, in Chita. In that time he'd been released and already got himself put away again. He was transported 650 kilometres from his camp to take part in my trial and give evidence against me. Remarkably he never did appear in the courtroom.

The Down-and-out

They brought him in and shoved him into the cell. He was a terrible sight, with a face the colour of mud, hands still black even after decontamination, and a thicket of hair that seemed to stick out uniformly all over his face and head. You couldn't get a good look at his eyes as they were swollen, either from a beating or a beating combined with a hangover. He looked, at first glance, about sixty to sixty-five years old. He shuffled in, peering around, and wound his way to the bed which one of us pointed out to him.

The old man unrolled the mattress, collapsed on to it and stayed there in silence for almost two days, getting up only for inspections and to go to the toilet. Nobody bothered him. On the third day he finally got up for the gruel as well. At which point we tried to engage him in conversation, but his unintelligible answers revealed nothing except what he'd been put inside for – hooliganism. The usual story.

Ignoring, as always, the Federal Penal Enforcement Service's misanthropic ban on sharing things, we gave him some tracksuit trousers, a jacket, underwear and a razor, supplemented his gruel with a few extras from our food parcels, and then forgot about the old man. After all, everyone has his own business to get on with, and it's a big cell.

Another week went by. One day I got back from a meeting with my lawyers and saw a newcomer – someone about my own age who'd clearly not had an easy life but looked pretty robust – busily tinkering with our television, having taken the back off it. I got a sinking feeling in my stomach. The television in our cell barely had a functioning picture but you could at least hear the news – and for me the news is my life.

'Who's this?' I groaned.

'Meet Valentin Ivanovich,' my cellmates responded. 'Remember the old guy? It's him. He's a radio technician. He says he can fix it.'

Valentin Ivanovich didn't turn round but nodded and continued with the job, kitted out as he was with a sharpened spoon and paperclips.

A few days later we got talking. His was a familiar story: his son was killed, then his wife died, he started drinking heavily, his devious neighbours got him kicked out of his apartment, he lived on the streets for nearly a year, got into a fight – and was brought in. Later I had a chance to look at his case file – the same story, just written in officialese.

He was pleasant to talk to, although we had very little time together because the court cases and the vast quantity of documents I had to read left only a tiny window of opportunity. He too was always busy, fixing things, equipping the cell in one way or another. The cell had clearly become his new home. And when, during my hunger-strike, the administration tried to get him to sign a false document saying that the hunger-strike hadn't taken place, like the rest of my cellmates he refused to do so, despite coming under significant pressure.

However, it became clear that he totally lacked the will

or readiness to fight for his own fate – so crucial if you're to keep your head above water in today's cruel world. His future was not hard to predict: prison – street – prison – death in a ditch from exposure or heart attack.

I have seen so many people like him over these years. And so often have I subsequently heard that they have died . . .

So then, what do you think? Is it not worth trying to make our world just a bit less cruel? After all, these people need only a very small bit of help . . .

Soon afterwards I was summoned to 'have a chat' with the prison governor and when I returned the cell was empty. They gave me fifteen minutes to get my things ready – I was being moved to a new prison.

I was leaving without saying goodbye, but having watched the latest REN-TV news – on a television that was now working pretty well.

The Aggrieved

In prison they're also called 'the dropouts', the 'downcast' and a whole litany of other far less savoury names. They are the prison's 'caste of untouchables': you don't sit at the same table as them, eat from the same dish, use the same utensils, and so on. In any disagreement within the prison community, their voice carries no weight whatsoever; as such they're unable to count on any form of protection.

Nowadays, thankfully, such distinctions are gradually eroding but much remains as it always was. Prison is a very conservative place.

In the world outside people generally think that it's only homosexuals and those who have committed the most depraved crimes like rape or child abuse who find themselves in this position.

That hasn't been the case for a long time. Nobody believes the courts any more, and anyone can claim that their sentence is just another result of coming into conflict with someone else's commercial interest. It's not easy to verify, and there are indeed a great number of cases relating to these 'commercial' issues.

There are not many genuine homosexuals in prison, so those who find themselves in the 'aggrieved' category are generally people who are unable to stand up for themselves, who have shown some form of weakness. And it is they who are forced to carry out all kinds of unpleasant work.

But sometimes it can turn out differently.

Ostap is one of the dozen or so 'aggrieved' who live in our barracks. A barracks is one large communal space – everything and everyone is on permanent view. Ostap didn't seem particularly different. A small, quiet guy who, like the rest of his 'caste', did the cleaning, took out the rubbish and washed other people's clothes. Nowadays, at least, this type of work is paid for in tea, cigarettes and the like.

Showing an interest in how someone came to be in this position is just not done.

Self-respecting detainees try to have a normal sort of relationship with the 'aggrieved', and avoid being discourteous, but those who feel that life has dealt them a raw deal and are more arrogant often look to bolster their own self-esteem by denigrating this defenceless group.

One day Ostap was just getting on with tidying up under a bed when a loutish bloke blatantly poked him below the waist as he went past, accompanying this distinctly offensive gesture with a no less offensive comment.

It was a run-of-the-mill occurrence, and usually the 'aggrieved' put up with it. And so Ostap, without standing up straight, muttered something quietly under his breath and moved slowly into the nearest corner.

Some halfwits standing a little way off started

sniggering; to hear what Ostap was muttering you had to stand pretty close to him. He was repeating just one phrase: 'I'll kill you.'

When, half a minute later, Ostap finally stood up straight, in his hand was an enormous shank he'd pulled out from somewhere – a thirty-centimetre-long piece of file, sharpened to be as lethal as a dagger.

I literally leapt out of the way. I had no desire whatsoever to get a piece of forged steel like that in my side.

But Ostap was already heading towards his tormentor. The latter made a dash for the only door, but this was blocked by a surge of people racing for the exit – also keen to avoid getting caught up in the heat of the moment. The rest just stood there, petrified.

Ostap moved slowly but deliberately, and his opponent began to howl. That's the only way to describe the drawn-out, bloodcurdling cry of a man who had just a few seconds left to live.

At this point we pulled ourselves together. Someone also screamed, someone, more cool-headed, moved the beds, preventing Ostap from reaching his target. His friends jumped in, grabbed him by the arms, dragged him off . . .

The reprieved victim eventually broke out of the barracks. He didn't come back – 'abandoning the detachment as a safety precaution'. A humiliating turn-of-phrase for the camp . . .

The following day Ostap was cleaning out the barracks once again, but people looked at him differently from then on. And when the regional prosecutor visited the camp for an inspection and invited anyone who wanted to meet him on a one-to-one basis (and this can be fraught with consequences), nobody was surprised when the only person who marched across the apparently deserted camp was Ostap.

'*Our* Ostap', as he was now called in the detachment, with a note of pride.

Roma

Half the criminals freed on parole return to the familiar world of the labour camp.

Every morning in our barracks starts with the deafening sound of an alarm and a wild screech.

If you think that a yell of almost a hundred decibels can't have any meaningful content, you're sorely mistaken.

The person doing the yelling is Roma, the night-time orderly. His job is to get everyone up. And he does so with considerable inventive aplomb. The melody emitted under his direction from an ordinary bell, and the words that go with it, are different virtually every time. Sometimes the gags are so good you just can't get up from laughing so hard.

Roma even looks like something from a gothic fable: sturdy, not very tall, with expressive, laughing eyes and a smile that reveals a single tooth in the middle of an otherwise empty mouth.

It was the booze that put Roma in jail. Whether it was just a fight or a robbery during a fight – he's none too clear. 'I don't remember' is all he can say.

Roma is making an effort to 'get back on track' and wants to apply for parole. Working as an orderly should help.

Occasionally I tease him. 'Why do you want to get out?

It's pretty good here – there's food, protection, you're kept off the booze . . .'

Roma is suddenly serious; he talks wistfully of how he'll get out, fix his teeth, get a job at the local factory. He can rely on that . . .

The seriousness disappears as quickly as it came on, and he skips off to do a session on the horizontal bars, where he also performs wonders.

Then comes the court hearing. It's a positive result. Ten days till freedom. Roma doesn't know what to do with himself. From time to time he comes up to me and describes in detail, day by day, what he'll do 'beyond the fence'. I listen attentively. He obviously needs to get it out of his system, but I know the statistics only too well: 50 per cent come back for another 'stay'.

Roma can sense my scepticism and tries passionately to convince me: 'I'm not coming back here again, ever!'

I pull his leg: 'Roma, at least try to get those teeth done.' For which I'm subjected to another detailed repetition of his plans.

Release day. Roma's somehow found himself a tracksuit and trainers, and he walks along the detachment yard followed by good wishes and goodbyes.

A month passes, and then another. No news from Roma. Some of the guys are starting to get seriously worried – they gave him money and are waiting for the packages they ordered.

Soon, however, word comes through. With a new intake of prisoners sent from a local prison. Alas, Roma is already there. He got drunk, got in a fight, nicked a phone. The town is small – he was recognized, of course, and arrested.

Why on earth did he do it? Who knows? Most likely he just didn't know what to do with himself and subconsciously wanted to return to the familiar world of the labour camp.

Sometimes you get the feeling that the police and the courts are playing a strange kind of game, by releasing on parole just the sort of people who they know they'll soon be locking up again. And they do absolutely nothing on the other side of the prison fence to make this a less frequent, or even less immediate, occurrence.

The explanation, of course, is simple: human beings are actually less than nothing for the state – they're just statistical report fodder.

As for the teeth, Roma didn't have time to get them fixed . . .

Betrayal

In the camp – as, in fact, on the other side of the barbed wire as well – it's usually older people who are the readers. The younger ones prefer to watch television – music videos mostly.

That's what made the young guy, with his head constantly in a book, stand out – that and his good-natured, cheeky grin.

In every other way he was unremarkable. Just another young lag with an alert look and a couple of tattoos (probably a souvenir from the juvenile penal colony; 'getting inked' is no longer popular in the adult prisons).

He happened to come up to me one day, asked if I had a book he could read. I learned that Lyosha (as the lad was called) loved fantasy. He'd finished school and was now in prison under Article 158 – for theft. He and some mates had done the rounds of empty dachas, and got caught. And then got caught again. So yes, he had indeed been in the juvenile colony. He'd turned eighteen in there, was transferred here to see out his sentence. Two years in this place already; he was soon due for early release on parole.

One day I noticed that, instead of reading as usual, Lyosha was pacing nervously up and down the barracks, occasionally waving his arms in despair as if engaged in some intractable conversation with someone.

I went up to him.

'What's happened?'

'Problems with the parole.'

'What kind of problems?'

There are generally two types of issues relating to conditional early release in the camps (if you discount corruption, which is both a problem and a solution). First, early release becomes much more difficult if you've tangled with the administration. Secondly, there's an illegal practice whereby the Federal Penal Enforcement Service assumes the role of the court and sets additional restrictions on early release depending on the crime for which the prisoner has been convicted.

But neither situation applied in this case. Both detainee and case were entirely unexceptional.

'So what problems are there?' I asked him.

And at this Lyosha suddenly broke down and the whole story came pouring out.

His father drank. He'd died not long ago. His mother drank. She was 'deprived of parental rights'. He and his two sisters were taken into temporary care. Then his mother had a cancer operation. She stopped drinking. She took her daughters back but he had to go to an orphanage. For Lyosha it was a stab-wound to the heart.

After the orphanage he ended up in the juvenile colony. His sisters have grown up, they're now over eighteen. His mother's still alive. Everything's okay. Six months ago they promised to come and visit him. He spent a week running round trying to find a room for the visit. By hook or by crook he managed to persuade a fellow inmate to let him have his reserved meeting slot (getting a room in the colony is no easy matter).

Then he waited. And waited. On visiting days, from the moment he wakes a prisoner's like a cat on hot bricks – the only comparable feeling is the day of release. But they didn't come to see Lyosha that day. A week later they told him on the phone that for some reason it just hadn't worked out.

Another stab-wound to the heart.

And now, early release on parole. For that to happen, our bureaucratic police state requires you, the prisoner behind bars, to provide documents (even if they're completely fictitious) proving that you have somewhere to live and a job on the outside.

Lyosha asked his mother and sisters to help. They said they were too busy.

'I've nowhere to go, and no reason to go anywhere,' was Lyosha's summing up of the situation.

I understood what he was going through. The documents weren't the issue. You can easily get someone to cobble them together – your former cellmates will do it. No, Lyosha had nothing to hold on to in life. No girlfriend, let alone a wife. How could he have? He'd been in prison since he was sixteen or seventeen. He'd lost his father, and now his mother and sisters had rejected him as well.

There was nothing to say, except the usual, 'Hang on in there, pal.'

And, though I'm ashamed to admit it, I felt a deep sense of joy that I didn't have to cope with this kind of betrayal. That there were people on the outside who loved me and were waiting for me.

Just think how many abandoned young men are languishing in Russia's prisons! How many of them there are in here only because they were desperately looking for someone to pay them some attention, craving a place in a world where they seemed like strangers even to those closest to them.

Lyosha wandered around for another day. Then he got into a scrap with another detainee over some minor issue. He had to do a week of 'additional labour duty'. He then got himself together and wrote a letter to his friends asking them to send the documents he needed.

Everything, it seemed, had resumed its normal course.

Except now Lyosha hardly ever smiles.

The Nazi

You certainly have some surprising encounters in prison. It so happened that most of the prisoners at my work-station were immigrants from Tadzhikistan and Kyrgyzstan. They speak Russian but prefer their own language, of course. So not wanting to be a nuisance (since, when I'm around, they politely try not to switch language), I sit myself next to a tall guy, who's swarthy and dark-haired like most of them, but who obviously prefers to speak Russian – clearly his first language.

The young man turns out to be half-Lithuanian, from Novosibirsk. And a real-life Nazi – that's to say he's a member of one of Russia's numerous National-Socialist groups. Alexander, as he was called, told me that the camp has 'only' twelve Nazi prisoners. They were all convicted for crimes committed as teenagers, which is why they've ended up in the general prison regime. He himself made bombs, and that's what he was sent down for – though there were other things, too, hence his long sentence: seven years. He's been doing time since he was seventeen; he's now nineteen.

Alexander is no fool; he got through his secondary school exams (in prison), is interested in philosophy and politics, wants to teach later on. He doesn't smoke, and says that he doesn't drink.

The work we do is tedious and doesn't stop us from

talking. What's more, I'm interested. I've never been able to understand how Nazism could be a phenomenon in a country where so many people lost their lives fighting it. I ask a few questions. Alexander is happy to answer them, at least as far as his general understanding and awareness allow him.

He got himself involved with a National-Socialist cell at thirteen: just saw a notice pinned up in a stairwell and gave them a call. He reveres Hitler as the standard bearer for white racial supremacy. He doesn't consider black or yellow people (redskins somehow don't come into it) as fully fledged human beings. For some reason he puts immigrants from Central Asia and the Northern Caucasus in the same category.

He doesn't believe in the Holocaust or the concentration camps. He's read all the relevant literature. He doesn't show any particular enmity towards the Jews, just disdain (as if to say, look at all the bogeymen they've managed to come up with). He enjoys telling me about the SS death marches in the Baltic states, shows me his swastika tattoo.

His girlfriend, too, is a Nazi. They met through one of the relevant websites, when he was on bail pending trial. They plan to get married.

The conversation is made all the more surreal by what's going on around us. Every so often there's a yell in accented Russian from one of our work-station colleagues: 'Hey, Sasha – another box.' Alexander carefully hands over a packed box, and himself requests, 'More paper.' There's no doubt our co-workers can hear what we're talking about, and now and again they throw in a good-natured comment.

*Sasha, I ask, so what are you going to do with the immigrants? –
Deport them.*

And the economy? – We'll nationalize it.

Who's going to do all the work? – The Russians.

And head up the businesses? – Committed National Socialists.

*But where are you going to find enough good specialists with
National-Socialist ideas? – We'll nurture them.*

Economics, by the way, isn't Sasha's strong point, and
after two or three hours of unhurried conversation he
clearly begins to see that National-Socialist ideas on the
economy are going nowhere. I reassure him with the
thought that liberals welcome pretty much any experiment
with socio-economic structures, offering as an example the
Israeli kibbutz and recommending that they too try out
their economic theories on small voluntary communities.

We then turn to a more contentious issue – that of
nationality, or, more precisely, race. There is no common
ground of understanding on this one.

*Sasha, what if your granddaughter was black, do you mean you
couldn't love her? – I'm not going to have a black granddaughter!*

*But Sasha, what if it just happened like that? Who knows
what the grandmother of your future son's intended might have
been? – I'm not going to have a black granddaughter!* Okay. A
dead end.

On the whole Sasha isn't an obstinate person, but on this
one emotions have evidently clouded his logic. Never mind,
we'll come back to it later.

I tackle the issue from another angle. I try to clarify his
vision for the existence of a nation of whites surrounded
by those of mixed race. It's fairly quickly clear that he

doesn't have such a vision, and I'm treated to a discourse on Hitler's successful conquest of Europe.

It's worth noting the extent to which Hitler is idolized as a man, and the SS and Gestapo as organizations. I remind him about Hitler's friendship with the Japanese – the 'yellows' (in Nazi terminology). This gives him pause, before he comes back with: 'Well, they're not completely yellow.'

I agree that this approach could be helpful. The Japanese and Chinese are not completely yellow; Africans and African-Americans aren't completely black, and so on. We both laugh.

We move on to the Holocaust. 'There was no Holocaust' – Sasha is unshakeable. He's read a book about the concentration camps; it said that the crematoria didn't have the capacity to process that many bodies. The same thing with the gas chambers. And in general it just wasn't 'like that' in the concentration camps.

Sasha, I say, I personally knew several concentration camp survivors. I met the first one in 1978 – I was fifteen, he was fifty, so it wasn't as if he was losing his marbles. He came to my school, gave a talk. And the most recent of my concentration camp acquaintances – Tom Lantos – died not long ago. And they all say the same thing: it happened!

In prison you never cast doubt on first-hand testimony. It's one of the worst insults. Sasha goes quiet. It's difficult for him. I can understand that.

The National-Socialist community had given the kid a sense of security, of being part of a team with a defined role, a sense of being part of something bigger than himself. They worked out together, went to football matches together, took on other gangs of (often ethnic) youths together. And it was there, amongst 'his own', that he met the girl who will soon be his wife. What's more, his comrades-in-arms from various cities even write to him in prison. He's not forgotten.

And Hitler? What about Hitler? For my generation – Alexander's parents' generation – he's an enemy of the human race. But for many of today's sixteen-to-twenty-year-olds, he's simply a historical figure, like Genghis Khan. And this is a problem only of the last few years: there are vanishingly few Nazis over the age of twenty-five.

A state that crushes society and stakes everything on the dehumanization of its people does resolve some of its ongoing political problems. Competition for power is weakened. Bureaucracy is able to take advantage of universal apathy and arbitrary political control. But 'when a country turns too grey, the brown will always come out' (Arkady and Boris Strugatsky, *Hard to be a God*). And so it has come to pass. And it has spattered our children with a vile, stinking slurry.

As for Sasha, we can still fight to keep him. We're no worse than today's Germans after all. And they've pretty much managed to deal with the problem there . . .

The Suicide

Tall, skinny, with sloping shoulders – the immediate impression was one of utter dejection. His story, though not an untypical litany of vicissitudes by prison standards, was also desperately sad.

He worked as a civil engineer. He'd been employed by a newly formed company, with responsibility for deliveries and the quality of construction – a good position and a decent salary. For eight months, while all the preliminary work was going on, everything went fine. Then his boss went on leave, and his deputy fell ill. Artyom (as our new cellmate was called) was asked to stand in for the bosses for a couple of weeks. At this point he became aware that nobody had ordered in the construction materials. Somewhat alarmed, he kept trying to contact the boss, but he was never in. His deputy was likewise unavailable. He went to the police, but they told him to get lost.

Shortly afterwards he started getting calls from anxious investors. Not only had the firm's managers disappeared without trace, so too had eight million dollars.

The very same policeman who had refused to deal with his earlier allegation now demanded a million roubles, or else he'd make sure the buck stopped with Artyom. Clearly he'd kept that promise. Artyom got eight years. His car and many of his possessions were confiscated 'to pay for the lawsuit'. His wife came to see him only once. The conversation didn't exactly flow.

You feel sorry for the guy, but in this place every other person has exactly the same story. You simply don't have the energy or time to listen to other people's woes. Every day there are court hearings, another stack of papers you have to read through. You just don't have the time for him! And yet he doesn't seem to understand this. He goes around whining on about how hopeless he feels, how the judge couldn't care less whether he was guilty or not, how his children are too ashamed to look him in the eye because 'Dad's a swindler who robbed people', how the truth is irrelevant if you haven't the money for a bribe . . .

Come on, we all know this already, and plenty more besides! It's not exactly earth-shattering news. Your own misery is always greater, obviously, but what's that got to do with anyone else?! Anyone will lend you a hand with the everyday stuff, but as for the mental anguish – sorry, pal, you just have to learn to deal with that yourself . . .

Prison has taught me to sleep lightly, so the throaty gurgling in the toilets wakes me instantly. I jump up, fling myself at the door, yank at it so that it bursts open – oh woe!

The light-bulb on the toilet wall is protected by a heavy-duty grille, some two and a half to three metres above the floor. Attached to this grille I see a cord made out of a torn bed-sheet, and hanging from the cord – Artyom. By the look of it, he's clambered on to the toilet and jumped off, but the cord has stretched a bit and so his feet – the very tips of his toes – are just touching the ground as the rope bounces up and down.

He's wheezing, clearly no longer aware of what's happening. I dash towards him and grab him, lifting him up with one hand and attempting to pull the cord off with the other. I can't do it. You wouldn't think he'd be that heavy but he's like a dead weight and I just can't lift him.

Grabbing him with both hands I just manage to hoist him up a little so that he can breathe, and I then call in a hoarse whisper (so that security don't come running): 'Guys, help me!'

This minute locked in an embrace with a semi-corpse feels like one of the longest in my life.

At last the others wake up, rush over and together we pull him out of the noose. We lay him down, press down on his chest – he starts to breathe, coughs, throws up. Okay, he's alive.

In the morning we give him a scarf to wrap around his neck, but the screws inevitably notice the circular bruise and soon Artyom is summoned 'with his belongings'.

The administration has no truck with suicides. They mess up the statistics. A failed attempt means the cooler, the 'attempted suicide' mark on your chest, and no early parole.

As for the rest of us, we avoided each other's eyes, ashamed. After all, we could have known that he was on the edge, but we chose to ignore it. Indifference is a terrible sin. It's only one short step away from the professional fish-eyed look of the unscrupulous judge who believes that the happiness of his own family is justification enough for any such 'Artyoms'.

Can we really be at peace with ourselves, pretending that someone else's fate is no concern of ours? How long can a country survive when indifference becomes the norm?

The time of reckoning always comes eventually.

The Rat

Small and balding, with dark, almost jet-black eyes, agile but somehow always on edge, N. N. found a permanent berth in the detachment's kitchen, officially called the 'mess room'.

It's here that you can come after work to have some tea and heat up a simple sandwich in the microwave – if there's anything to make one with. Though, in fact, a piece of bread from the canteen, slightly heated up, isn't bad on its own.

Then there are those who have it rather better: regular parcels, the chance to purchase more than the usual pitiful amount allowed from the shop. Anything is possible if you have a profession, if you work, if your family hasn't forgotten about you.

And of course, although it's officially forbidden, 'resources' get shared around. Things are shared with a friend, or the person sitting next to you at the table or sleeping in the adjacent bunk; or else you get your laundry done or something mended in exchange for food.

Working in the kitchen isn't the most prestigious job but it pays. You wipe the tables, fetch the boiling water, wash the dishes, cut the sausage. And the many other things people don't want to do after a trying day. And in return people will always ask you to share a cup of tea, give you some sweets or sugar, or cut you a piece of the sausage they've received from home.

In fact most of the food is kept right here under the control of N. N., whose job it is to remember what belongs to whom, where it is, and whose stuff is kept with whose, so that no one can make off with somebody else's by mistake. So when I find myself being treated to my own coffee, which I immediately recognize by its taste, I'm a little surprised.

'Where did you get this?'

'N. N. gave it to me, or to be precise swapped it for some fags. Why?'

'It's my coffee, and I haven't shared it with anyone yet.'

'I smell a rat . . .'

Accusing someone of stealing from fellow inmates is, according to prison tradition, one of the most serious accusations you can make. Being labelled a 'rat' is not a situation you ever want to find yourself in. And the reason is clear: this is an enclosed group of men, there's a lot of pent-up aggression around. Mutual suspicion quickly leads to bitter conflict. The enquiry is swift and exhaustive.

The suspect's locker is broken open. The container found in the locker is carefully compared with the one I bring out of my bag. There can be no doubt. All his personal stuff gets checked out. There's a pile – literally a pile – of food in there. It all gets laid out for people to see and recover what belongs to them – this doesn't take long.

A lot of terse remarks.

'I was wondering where that had got to.'

'There, you see, you shouldn't have picked on me after all . . .'

The only item that's not found is a very conspicuous box of 'Moscow' sweets given to someone by his wife and now, as a result of this 'inspection', found to be missing from his bag. Yet another rat?!

A couple of hours later N. N. is summoned, with his 'belongings'. He's getting transferred to another detachment. The administration has its own informers and its own understanding of the risks of leaving a rat among an irate 'community'. A pretty acute understanding, in fact.

There's one final search before he's transferred. Lo and behold – the Moscow sweets. Sewn into the sleeve of his jacket!

When did he manage to do that? We just keep silent and exchange a few looks.

That evening we get into a heated discussion: why did he need all that stuff? He couldn't have eaten it. It was obviously going to be discovered sooner or later. And it's not as if he was hungry – everyone was always sharing things with him. No one refused when he asked. Was he a klepto? Didn't seem to be. It was a mystery . . .

On the other hand, when you think about the way things are in our country now, you come across this type of mystery all the time. The pilfering just keeps on going. People buy islands and vast impersonal villas, they build dozens of palaces and fleets of yachts, they stuff their garages full of expensive cars they can't drive anywhere, and their coffers with jewellery they're probably too ashamed to wear. It's as if they intend to live for ever. As if they don't understand that you can't hide all this stuff or justify it on any salary.

Kleptomania then?

Or do they get a bogus sense of stability from accumulating such a vast quantity of things?

Perhaps they're simply fools? More foolish still is the idea that 'this lot have already stolen just about everything, so better to keep the devil we know!'

You wouldn't hear this said in the camp barracks. Here people know for sure that a rat won't stop, you have to deal with him, humanely or not.

It's very strange to expect anything positive to come from 'stability', when the entire political regime is gradually turning into a nest of greedy, vile rats.

The Father

He was the quarantine overseer. There's a separate building where all new arrivals are quarantined for the first week or two to check for any infectious diseases and to find out 'what makes them tick'. From here they then get assigned to a particular detachment. And, in fact, how your life works out in prison can pretty much hinge on the results of the quarantine inspection. So they tend to make only serious, reliable people overseers. I might add that there is also something called 'red quarantine', but that's another discussion entirely, and probably best conducted with a criminal investigation team. I've been fortunate enough to avoid this experience.

He introduced himself as Konstantin. Older than many fellow lags, well over forty, thick-set and with a calm look in his almost jet-black eyes. We shook hands. It can get pretty boring in the quarantine block – most of the detainees they bring in are young. We gradually got talking.

Konstantin was a professional driver, but he'd spent his whole life working with sheep. He'd been tending the flocks at the local state farm. These flocks, some 9,000 strong, belonged to the state. Konstantin had been selling lambs on the side. When they caught up with him, he admitted everything. The loss was calculated at a million roubles, and he was offered the chance to repay it – but he refused. He got nine years. He had already done six and was getting ready for conditional release on parole.

'They've told me they're going to let me out.'

'So, was it worth it?' I asked.

'Of course' – not a moment's doubt. 'My daughter's now at school in St Petersburg. A straight-A student. Where would she have gone otherwise? To work at the uranium-enrichment plant? No way! My wife and I are happy for her.'

'What are you going to do?'

'They'll take me on as a driver again, I was promised. They know that I won't touch anyone else's stuff, everything's privatized now, the owners are locals, our people. You don't steal from your own, that's about as low as it gets.'

'What about going to St Petersburg, to your daughter?'

'How would my wife and I do that? We don't have that kind of money, anyway it's too late.'

We sit there drinking our tea. Two men no longer young, who have both made a choice to go to prison. Loved ones are waiting for us at home, and we're here, and it's our decision. Was it the right one – who knows? I'm certainly not the one to judge Konstantin . . .

The Addict

There was something totally dejected about him. Tall, nearly two metres in height, skinny and stooping, his nose badly broken, with small eyes, and huge swollen hands on long arms – hands that you couldn't fail to notice immediately – Oleg was always to be found standing on the first floor of the barracks.

In fact, that's what everyone called him – 'First Floor'.

'Hey, First Floor, where's Abdulayev? They're looking for him!'

'First, the inspector's coming. Let everybody know!'

'Tell the supply officer to come over, will you, First . . .'

And so it would continue, all day long. The duty orderly's assistant, a human walkie-talkie . . .

Things had been a bit different before, however. The first-floor position had been occupied by a professional grass, who had no compunction in planting a prohibited item (like a shank, a homemade knife) in the bedside table of anyone who crossed his path – and then tipping off the detention officer that he might want to do a 'thorough inspection'.

This guy had felt he was the 'floor boss', and he'd yell and lash out at fellow prisoners, who couldn't respond. He didn't have the sense, however, to know where to draw the line. There was a ferocious, short-lived fight; he was sent to the punishment ward and then transferred to another detachment.

And now, Oleg. Quiet, diligent, but utterly opposed to mistreating anyone or informing on them.

One day we were out shovelling snow together. We got talking.

He's thirty. Already a veteran drug addict. He's had AIDS for several years but his immunity is still holding up, although he constantly gets weeping sores on his legs. Before prison he worked as a meat cutter. He liked his job, the money wasn't bad. Enough to be able to buy drugs.

His intake increased. He had to switch to worse quality drugs. When they busted him he was immediately charged with possession because of the quantity. They beat him up badly, but he didn't grass up his supplier. And so he was put away.

His partner also has AIDS. She's an orphan. He's only got his mother. She used to earn pretty good money, enough to get by. But now his mother's fallen ill and things are very tight. His mother lives with his partner, who is 170 centimetres tall and weighs just 45 kilos. She's very worried that she won't last until his release.

When I ask him why he doesn't take any medication, Oleg reveals a toothless grin.

'If you start taking the medication you have to carry on. Or else it only makes you worse. My family can't afford to buy it, it's very expensive. But to get the free stuff – half the year it's there, half the year it isn't. When I get out, though . . .'

And then, under his breath: 'If she lasts that long . . .'

'So how did it come to this, Oleg, why did you fritter your life away like this? Why didn't you quit the drugs?'

'I tried to quit, several times. But then my mates would come along and it would all start off again . . . I don't have the strength any more. When I get out, I've got to get away. But where do I go? And how? What about my mother, my partner . . .'

He sighs and carries on shovelling snow that falls like an endless shroud. A gangly, sad figure against a white swirling background.

It Will Come Back to Haunt You

Criminal behaviour in Russia's labour camps is generally divided into 'red' and 'black' types. Both rely on a close partnership between the administration and the criminals, each pursuing their own – often entirely self-serving – interests. In the 'black' camps it's usually a question of money from drug dealing, while in the 'red' it's extortion. There are, of course, plenty of exceptions to this rule.

The methods of applying pressure are not stunningly original: beatings of varying degrees of intensity and seriousness. Usually it's the prisoners themselves who do the beating, tacitly encouraged by the administration. Although the prison employees also like a bit of a 'workout' now and then.

To get early conditional release on parole you have to pay, whichever camp you're in.

The claim that in the black camps it's the criminal 'authorities' who run the show, in opposition to the administration, is no longer true – and hasn't been for some time. The differences, on the whole, are strictly aesthetic: in the red camps there is a certain outward show of discipline while in the black there are unspoken rules, a prevailing 'ideology'. And, while the administration is very visible in the red camps, in the black it hides behind the criminal element.

Over the last few years the situation has been gradually changing. 'Black' and 'red' are giving way to 'bureaucratic' criminality, which is the norm throughout the country. As physical violence has decreased, there has been an increasing tide of paperwork, regulations and selective application of the law. In other words the law is still not regarded as 'gospel', but at least people aren't getting crippled so much.

Vyacheslav is a sturdy fellow with fiery red hair, around thirty-five to forty years old. He's been inside a long time – since 2002. He used to be a member of a vicious local gang but the authorities couldn't pin any murders on him, so having knocked out most of his teeth they put him away for extortion.

In prison Vyacheslav began to cooperate with the administration, and as a trusted representative he was given the job of handling my 'adaptation'. The standard procedure for putting a new arrival in his place wasn't going to work with me, as might be expected – after all, beating wasn't allowed, I knew the laws better than most, and early release wasn't exactly likely. So after a couple of days we moved on to having some heart-to-heart conversations.

I'd long ago worked out my own script for these encounters, but it's very interesting to listen to what a typical 'red camp' inmate has to say. His words reveal an unconcealed, genuine hatred for those who have ruined his life – both the criminal fraternity and the authorities.

He's reluctant to talk much about his past in the camp, but on the whole he's honest.

'Did you beat people up?'

'Well, these days, of course, it's all "Would you be so kind as to . . .", but in the past, yes, I beat people up . . . How could you refuse? They call you in and say "Go and deal with him." If you don't, you know they'll give you the full treatment in the isolation cell.'

'Did you enjoy beating people?'

'Of course I didn't. I can resolve it without violence but they don't understand that, they'll say you're a wimp. A lot of them, though, do enjoy it. The feeling of power . . .'

'And what about later, on the outside? After all, you could bump into someone you've done over.'

'Could do. And it does happen. Not to everyone, of course. When these guys are released they get taken out of the camp in a bread truck, driven straight to the train. But in any case they'll find them. It's just that they only start thinking about that a couple of months before they're let out. They're thick-headed . . .'

Vyacheslav lets out a deep sigh, clenching and unclenching his fists with their battered knuckles. The conversation has clearly unsettled him. He's due out in a year himself . . .

And I can't help thinking of the thousands of people who are just like him, though to all appearances they're ordinary decent servants of the current regime. People who, in ten years' time at the most, will be grating their teeth and shaking in their boots as they realize that their time is over, and that criminal behaviour will always come back to haunt you in the long run.

The Thief

He answers to the name of Rustam, although his ID card says otherwise. However, this too is a lie: he's in prison under forged documents, something he doesn't try to hide.

He says that when he told the investigating cop that it wasn't his real name and that he'd already done time in Russia, the cop just flailed his arms at him and replied: 'Button it. Don't even think of telling the judge. They'll send your case back to me and I won't be able to go off on holiday . . .'

'And what was it to me?' Rustam shrugs. 'He didn't need the hassle, neither did I. So they convicted me as a "first-timer" which is why I ended up in here. If I'd known, I'd never have agreed to it.'

'What, you mean it's better in maximum security?'

'You bet,' he replies, his eyes half-closing at the pleasant recollection. 'Doing time in Krasnodar I had everything, I didn't want to leave. The warden even said as much: "Why take early parole, you've got everything you need here? Stay!" And so I stayed . . .'

Rustam's nationality is Tadjik; his profession – thief. It's a 'profession' he loves and you get the sense he wouldn't change it for anything. He's already nearly forty but this is only his second spell in prison. He got four years. He regards what happened as an acceptable 'professional risk'.

'In fact we get nabbed quite often,' he admits. 'After all, it's usually markets and warehouses we go for, the haul is fairly big. The patrol-guard police know where to wait for us. Generally we come to an agreement, but this time – it was my own stupid fault – I didn't bring any money with me. So I couldn't buy my way out of it. And they were rookies. If I'd known them I could have paid them off later. It was bad luck . . .'

Rustam, it seems, likes telling stories. He works next to me in the workshop. His stories relieve the boredom.

'Then there was the time we got a tip-off about a warehouse – we were told there was money in the safe. So we hire a pick-up and promise the driver we'll settle up after the job. When we break into the warehouse, what do we find? Eight safes. We load them all in. While we're at it we toss in a few crates of butter, honey, jam – whatever was in the warehouse. No point going off with a half-empty vehicle, right?'

Rustam gives me a questioning look. I can't help smiling. He's satisfied with my reaction.

'So we get to the destination, unload the safes; the driver's waiting on the street. We open the safes – there's no money. Not a brass farthing. Just some bits of paper and a few seals – complete garbage. We're thinking, how are we going to tell the driver, he'll never believe us. It has to be done, so I go out to where he's waiting. I tell him, look, this is how it is, the safes are empty, don't be mad at us, take the food. The driver nods, looks at me with pity, and says, "Well, you lot have had a tough night of it, take this," and hands me a few notes from his wallet. I take them and go back to the others. Those few thousand came in pretty handy, as it turned out.'

We both laugh.

'What will you do afterwards?'

Rustam makes no secret of it: 'I'll go back home, change my passport and then either head back to Moscow or make my way through Turkey to France. I know a lot of people there. They'll help me out.'

'In your previous "profession"?'

'What else can I do?'

A month later we say goodbye to each other. Rustam's getting early parole, he promises to write. And soon after, I do receive a brief letter from him, and a photograph of Rustam, happy with life, a few pounds heavier, some neat little houses behind him. And further beyond – the sea.

There's no return address, but he writes regularly to the guys and sends his greetings.

Amnesty

In prison and camp, amnesties are endlessly discussed, rumoured, anticipated. Even when there is no reason to assume that an amnesty is on the cards.

And when this sacred word is actually pronounced, out there 'on the outside', it creates an atmosphere of universal hope. Inmates latch on to every word heard from relatives or on the radio, and pass it on. Just let that day of freedom be brought closer, if only by a month or so.

After all, conditional early release on parole is far from being an option for everyone. It could be that there are ongoing legal claims against you, which you can't pay off; or the administration might be biased against you, particularly if you're seen as 'too clever by half'. Or the police or investigator who conducted your case might make an informal 'request' to deny release. Or else someone who doesn't want you to be on the outside just pays a simple back-hander. There are many ways to stymy you, to send you back to your seat 'until the bell goes'.

An amnesty is like waiting for a miracle to happen.

And then here it is! You get your hands on a draft of the proposed decree. You desperately search for your category of conviction to see whether it's been amnestied. You find it – oh joy! Hope made flesh in paper and ink. You start calling your relatives; they experience delight, mixed with anxiety. And then you wait.

It's only the old lags, whose lives can no longer brook illusion, who give a wry smile in answer to questions. So they are carefully given a wide berth. Scepticism is scary, even infuriating: how can you not believe in a miracle? Look, here it is, right in front of you: they've declared a 'sweeping amnesty', 150,000 people, it's going to impact on everyone to some extent, surely . . .

The big day arrives. Everyone stands frozen in front of the radio, listening.

No! This can't be! Not one person! Only 2,000 from all the camps?! And in any case that's just women, juveniles and invalids, and not many of them even . . . But what about us?! Are they really saying there's nothing, not even a day?! It can't be true . . .

The old-timers' eyes are sad. They don't take any satisfaction in being proved right. It's just the same as always. And as always they feel sorry for those who haven't yet learned 'not to believe'.

And then the call home is hard. To your mother, your wife. They already know, they understand everything. But you can't help feeling as though it's your fault that hope has been extinguished once again, and that years of separation still lie ahead.

Cruelty that begets cruelty. A society where goodness and empathy are seen as synonymous with madness. A country where people are no longer decapitated, nor, on the whole, martyred at the stake, but where we're still not prepared to fight for every single life, every individual fate.

Friends, fellow citizens, we're few and far between as it is, and every passing year we're getting fewer.

Don't you see, we're fading away . . .

Let's show some compassion for one another, while there's still someone to feel it for.

And one last thing.

Pick up the phone, give your parents a call.